THE BIG PLATINUM JUBILEE

The Great Monarch Of The UK, And All There Is To Know About

Queen Elizabeth II

John Hardman

INTRODUCTION

CHAPTER 1

HM The Queen
    Childhood
    A New Monarch Takes Her Place As Head Of State
    The monarchy of today

CHAPTER 2

Milestones Such As Anniversaries
    The Celebration of the Jubilee's 25th Anniversary
    The Celebration Of The Golden Jubilee
    Diamond Wedding Anniversary
    The Diamond Jubilee Anniversary
    The 80th Birthday Celebrations For Her Majesty Queen Elizabeth II

Her Majesty's 90th birthday celebrations
    Interests
    Monarchy's Longest Continuity

CHAPTER 3

Itinerary For The Platinum Jubilee Festivities

The 2nd of June
    Colorful Trooping
    Candles With A Platinum Jubilee

June 4th
    Epsom Downs Hosts The Derby.
    A Royal Platinum Ball at Buckingham Palace

On Sunday, June 5th.
    Jubilee Lunch, a Big Deal
    The Pageant of the Platinum Jubilee

Introduction

The reign of a king is marked by a number of notable events. Celebrations that are meaningful to the majority of people, like wedding anniversaries or birthdays, are included in this category, but the monarchy also has its own set of special anniversaries. In addition to the day they became king or queen, important dates include the accession anniversary, the coronation anniversary, and the so-called Jubilee celebrations.

Celebrations of a monarch's life and reign are known as jubilee anniversaries. Instead of occurring on a yearly basis, Jubilees are reserved for big anniversaries, elevating their significance. The term "Jubilee" is used to describe a specific period of time for each Jubilee:

- The Silver Jubilee commemorates the monarchy's 25-year reign.
- a 40th anniversary celebration

- Fifty years represents the Golden Jubilee began.
- a 60-year milestone
- 65th anniversary of the Sapphire Jubilee
- 70 years anniversary of platinum jubilee

After more than 200 years on the throne, George III became the first British king to celebrate his 50th birthday in 1809. There were formal services, a party, and a firework show to commemorate his Golden Jubilee.

In 1897, at the end of her 60-year reign, Queen Victoria became the first monarch to commemorate her Diamond Jubilee. The occasion was honored by a service of thanksgiving at St. Paul's Cathedral and a great procession through the streets of London, which were lined with well-wishers applauding for the Queen. "I believe no one ever, I believe, has met with such an ovation as was given to me, traveling through those 6 miles of streets," Victoria wrote in her notebook. The applause was thunderous, and everyone's expressions revealed genuine happiness. I was very moved and ecstatic'.

During her Golden Jubilee in 2002, and her Diamond Jubilee in 2012, Queen Elizabeth II marked her two-decade reign. Her Majesty The Queen will celebrate her Platinum Jubilee in 2022, making her the first British monarch to do so. The Queen's Diamond Jubilee will be marked by an extended bank holiday weekend, public events, beacon lighting, services, pageants, and many other festivities.

I have written in subsequent chapters all there is to know about Queen Elizabeth II and her Platinum jubilee celebration.

Chapter 1

HM The Queen

The Reigning Monarch Of Great Britain

Elizabeth Alexandra Mary, Queen Elizabeth II of the United Kingdom of Great Britain and Northern Ireland and her other realms and territories by the grace of God. Crown Princess Elizabeth II of the United Kingdom

The 21st of April, 1926 (age 96) London, United Kingdom

Dynasty: the Windsor family

The Duke and Duchess of Edinburgh's notable relatives include George VI, mother Elizabeth, daughter Anne, Prince Andrew, Duke of York, Prince Charles, Prince Edward, Earl of Wessex, Princess Margaret, and Prince Philip, Duke of Edinburgh.

In full regalia, Her Majesty Elizabeth Alexandra Mary, better known as Elizabeth II, was crowned the monarch of the United Kingdom of Great Britain and Ireland on April 21, 1926 and Northern Ireland on February 6, 1952, by the Grace of God. She is the current Queen, Head of the Commonwealth, and Defender of the Faith of the United Kingdom. In 2015, she became the longest-reigning queen in British history, beating out her predecessor, Queen Victoria.

Childhood

Her father, Prince Albert, Duke of York, and his wife Lady Elizabeth Bowes-Lyon were the parents of the elder Elizabeth. On December 11, 1936, when her uncle Edward VIII (then duke of Windsor) abdicated in her father's favor to become King George VI, she became the presumed heir to the throne as the only child of George V's younger son.

The education of the princess was overseen by her mother, who left the girls in the care of a governess named Marion Crawford. C.H.K. Marten, who would later become the provost of Eton College, also tutored the princess in history, and the princess also received lessons in music and foreign languages from visiting teachers. The assault on London was so intense that Princess Elizabeth and her sister, Princess Margaret Rose, were compelled to spend a great deal of time away in Balmoral Castle in Scotland, as well as the Royal Lodge in Windsor and Windsor Castle.

This trip to South Africa was made in early 1947, with the king and queen accompanying their daughter Princess Elizabeth. Her engagement to her distant cousin, Lieutenant Philip Mountbatten of the Royal Navy, previously Prince Philip of Greece and Denmark, was announced shortly after her homecoming.

On November 20, 1947, the couple married in Westminster Abbey. Prince Philip bestowed onto his son-in-law titles of dukedom Edinburgh, the earldom of Merioneth, and Baron Greenwich on him before their wedding. They settled in London's Clarence House. On November 14, 1948, at Buckingham Palace, Prince Charles and Lady Diana Spencer had their first child, Charles Philip Arthur George.

A New Monarch Takes Her Place As Head Of State

When King George VI's health began to deteriorate in the summer of 1951, Princess Elizabeth stepped in to represent him at the Trooping of the Colour and other official events. A successful tour of Canada and the United States culminated in a stay in New York City, Philadelphia, and DC on October 7. On the way to Australia and New Zealand in January 1952, she and the Duke of Edinburgh learned of the king's death in Sagana, Kenya, on February 6, 1952. Elizabeth, who was now queen, returned to England right away. The first three months of her reign were spent in relative solitude as she mourned the death of her father. Even after moving from Clarence House to

Buckingham Palace, she began performing the duties of a sovereign that fall, holding her first official opening of Parliament on November 4, 1952. Her coronation took place on June 2, 1953, at Westminster Abbey.

On their six-month Commonwealth tour, which began in November 1953, the queen and the Duke of Edinburgh made their first visits to Australia and New Zealand as a reigning British monarchs. She and the duke visited Canada and the United States in 1957 after making state visits to many European countries.

She was the first reigning British queen to visit South America (in 1968) and the Persian Gulf countries (since 1961), the first royal British tour to the Indian subcontinent in more than half a century (in 1979). It was in 1977, at her "Silver Jubilee," that she presided over a London banquet attended by 36 leaders of the Commonwealth, toured the UK and Northern Ireland, and traveled to the South Pacific and Australia, Canada, and the Caribbean.

Prince Charles was named Prince of Wales on July 26, 1958, and he was enthroned on July 1, 1969, following his mother's ascension to the throne. Other royal children include Princess Anne, born on August 15, 1950, and named princess royal in 1987; Prince Andrew named duke of York in 1986, and Edward named earl of Wessex and Viscount Severn in 1999.

Prince Andrew and Prince Edward were the only two boys born to Queen Elizabeth II, the third being Princess Diana, born on February 19, 1960. However, in 1960, Elizabeth chose to create the hyphenated name Mountbatten-Windsor for those descendants who weren't given the titles of prince or princess or royal highness. The birth of Princess Anne's son, Elizabeth's first grandchild, took place on November 15, 1977.

The monarchy of today

Even in the 1970s, when the royal family's private lives were televised and when her sister's marriage was officially annulled, Queen Elizabeth II looked to be increasingly aware of the modern role of the monarchy. It wasn't all plain sailing for the royal family in the 1990s. When Prince Charles and Diana divorced in 1992, Elizabeth referred to the year as the royal family's "annus horribilis." Prince Andrew and Sarah divorced in the same year.

In addition, Anne's marriage ended in divorce, and Windsor Castle was destroyed in a fire. As the kingdom went through a recession, public discontent with the royal family's lifestyle grew, and in 1992 Elizabeth, despite being free from paying taxes on her own income, consented to do so on behalf of the entire royal family. After the breakup of Charles and Diana in 1992 and their subsequent divorce in 1996, many people considered the royal family outdated and unfeeling.

After Diana's death in 1997, the criticism grew, especially after Elizabeth refused to allow Buckingham Palace to fly the national flag at half-staff. Later, the monarchy's image was updated to be less stuffy and formal, in keeping with the queen's previous efforts to modernize it. These endeavors had varying degrees of success.

During the 50th year of her reign, Elizabeth marked the occasion. Several days of celebrations in London were part of the "Golden Jubilee" events that took place around the Commonwealth. In the wake of the deaths of Elizabeth's mother and sister earlier in the year, the celebrations were a bit dimmer.

Even Charles's 2005 marriage to Camilla Parker Bowles received widespread support from the British people in the latter part of the first decade of the 21st century. Elizabeth presided over the family's celebration of Prince William of Wales's wedding to Catherine Middleton in April 2011.

She became the second-longest-reigning monarch in British history, after Victoria, the following month. Earlier this month, Elizabeth became the first British queen to visit Ireland since 1911 when she made a historic journey to the

Republic of Ireland. Queen Elizabeth II marked her 60th birthday in 2012 when she celebrated her "Diamond Jubilee." On September 9, 2015, she broke Queen Victoria's record of 63 years and 216 days in power as the longest-reigning monarch in history.

Prince Philip announced his retirement from public life in August of that year, but he continued to attend official engagements on a sporadic basis after that. Even while Prince Charles and other senior members of the royal family took on more responsibilities in Elizabeth's absence, the royal family's available substitutes diminished once Prince Harry and his wife, Meghan, decided to step down from their royal roles in March 2020.

The Crown, a Netflix series about the Windsors that premiered in 2016, sparked a surge in public interest in the queen and her family during this time period. Philip, Elizabeth's husband of more than seven decades, passed away in April of 2021 after a series of health problems. When Elizabeth and Philip celebrated their 50th wedding anniversary in 1997, she told him, "He has been my strength and stay all these years."

Aside from her customary and ceremonial obligations, Elizabeth is considered to have a serious and knowledgeable interest in government business. In her private life, she developed into something of a horsewoman, buying racehorses and visiting horse races as a spectator. She is one of the wealthiest women in the world because of her financial and real estate interests.

Did You Know?

1. In 1942, the Princess of Wales was made an honorary colonel of the Grenadier Guards, which she served with until her death in 1953.
2. During World War I, the British royal family took on the surname Windsor, which Queen Elizabeth II has proudly kept.
3. Elizabeth I's lace baptism gown was used to christen Princess Elizabeth.

Chapter 2

Milestones Such As Anniversaries

During the Queen's reign, a staggering amount of noteworthy occurrences have taken place. Every year since her coronation, Her Majesty has celebrated her jubilees and birthdays with delight and reflection. The Sovereign's importance in national identity and togetherness is reinforced as people across the Commonwealth gather together to celebrate a key occasion for their Head of State in these events.

The Celebration of the Jubilee's 25th Anniversary

In the year 1977, Celebrations for the Queen's Silver Jubilee took place across the United Kingdom and the Commonwealth.

In church services throughout the month of February, the anniversary of the Queen's accession on February 6, 1952, was celebrated. Jubilee celebrations began in late July 1977 with a family weekend at Windsor Castle, where the Queen stayed with her husband, Prince Philip, and their children.

On May 4th, the Queen received patriotic addresses from both chambers of Parliament and responded by emphasizing the jubilee's theme of national togetherness.

The Queen began on a large-scale trip throughout the summer months, having determined that she wanted to honor her jubilee by meeting as many of her people as she could. There has never been any monarch who covered so much ground in the United Kingdom in such a short time period; the six jubilee trips to the United Kingdom and Northern Ireland included stops in 36 different counties.

On the 17th of May, the first home tour began in Glasgow, which had never seen such a large crowd before. Thousands of people flocked to Lancashire, England, on one particular day for the tour, which ended with a stop in Northern Ireland.

There were also official abroad visits to Western Samoa, Australia, and New Zealand as well as Tonga, Fiji, and Tasmania. The Queen and the Duke of Edinburgh are expected to have traveled 56,000 miles this year.

The patriotic celebrations reached their peak in early June. The Queen ignited a bonfire beacon on Monday evening, June 6th, at Windsor, which set off a chain of beacons all around the country. Thousands of people lined the streets of London on Tuesday, June 7th, to see the Queen arrive at St Paul's Cathedral for a service of thanksgiving attended by international leaders and previous British prime ministers.

A luncheon in the Guildhall followed, where the Queen spoke afterward in front of guests including members of the Royal Family. At the age of 21, I made a promise to God that I would dedicate my life to serving the people of this city,' she said. That promise, which I made while I was still in my salad days, is one that I do not regret or rescind in any way.'

Hundreds of millions of people tuned in to see the procession make its way back down the Mall. The Queen made multiple balcony appearances at Buckingham Palace. All around the country, people began throwing block parties and village fairs; in London alone, 4,000 celebrations were said to have taken place.

On Thursday, June 9, a ceremonial barge trip down the Thames from Greenwich to Lambeth mimicked Elizabeth I's historic river journeys to cap off the main commemoration week. Afterward, the Queen returned to Buckingham Palace for more balcony appearances in front of a cheering throng after opening the Silver Jubilee Walkway and the new South Bank Jubilee Gardens. The tour concluded with a firework show.

There was a time in 1977 when the nation had an opportunity to express its love and gratitude for Her Majesty's 25 years of faithful devotion to the British monarchy. The Queen decided that the Appeal should focus on generating cash to support young people and, in particular, on encouraging and helping young people to serve others in the community. Grants of more than £80 million have been awarded by The Queen's Trust, formerly known as the Queen's Silver Jubilee Trust. Low-income areas are the focus of this program's educational and personal development efforts.

The Celebration Of The Golden Jubilee

In 2002, there was a flurry of celebrations to mark the Queen's 50th birthday. Celebration, community, service, past, and future, giving gratitude, and the Commonwealth were all-important Jubilee themes.

Throughout the year, the Queen and the Duke of Edinburgh traveled extensively throughout the Commonwealth and the United Kingdom.

She and her majesty toured every corner of the British Isles from Falmouth in Cornwall to the Isle of Skye during their tour.

No. 10 Downing Street for a supper hosted by Prime Minister David Cameron; Westminster Hall for an address by Her Majesty Queen Elizabeth II; and the Palace for a meeting of the Parliamentary Joint Committee. It was also attended by representatives of the Armed Services, who were given a banquet at Windsor Castle.

This Golden Jubilee means everything to me because of the people of this country and the Commonwealth, and because of the gratitude, respect, and pride, I feel for them.

A classical music concert in the gardens of Buckingham Palace kicked off the Jubilee celebrations in June 2002. Following a ceremonial procession from Buckingham Palace, there was a

Jubilee Church service in Windsor and a National Service of Thanksgiving at St Paul's Cathedral. A pop performance at Buckingham Palace featured Paul McCartney, Bryan Adams, Elton John, and Shirley Bassey as well as a host of other artists. With a stunning fireworks display and The Queen's final beacon, the National Beacon, being lit across the Commonwealth, the night came to a close.

On June 4, 2002, Her Majesty the Queen gave a speech at Guildhall in London thanking the people for their support throughout her reign:

"I'd like to express my gratitude to everyone here in Guildhall, on the Mall, and in the streets of London, as well as to anyone else watching on television in any part of the country or the Commonwealth. Thanks to everyone who helped us celebrate our 50th anniversary."

Diamond Wedding Anniversary

This past November 20, 2007, the Queen and the Duke of Edinburgh marked their 60th wedding anniversary together.

A service of celebration was held at Westminster Abbey, and a new Jubilee Walkway panoramic panel was unveiled in Parliament Square as part of the celebrations.

Prince Philip's uncle Earl Mountbatten's home, Broadlands in Hampshire, served as the backdrop for the pair as they recreated the honeymoon photos shot 60 years before.

The Diamond Jubilee Anniversary

With an extravagant core weekend and a series of regional visits across the United Kingdom and Commonwealth countries, the Diamond Jubilee was celebrated.

Queen Elizabeth II and Prince Philip visited every region of the United Kingdom in 2012 while members of the Royal Family toured the rest of the Commonwealth realms (countries in which the

Queen serves as head of state). There were visits to Australia, Canada, New Zealand, and Papua New Guinea, as well as Tuvalu, by the Prince of Wales and the Duchess of Cornwall and the Duke and Duchess of Cambridge.

On Saturday, Her Majesty the Queen paid a visit to the Epsom Derby, kicking off the key weekend. Sunday was a day of 'Big Jubilee Lunches' around the UK, where people were urged to gather with friends and neighbors to celebrate the Queen's Diamond Jubilee.

On Sunday, the Thames Diamond Jubilee Pageant featured up to 1,000 vessels from all across the United Kingdom, Commonwealth countries, and the world. The Queen and the Duke of Edinburgh boarded the Royal Barge, which served as the centerpiece of the flotilla's centerpiece.

As part of the BBC's Diamond Jubilee celebrations on Monday, a number of celebrities gathered at Buckingham Palace for a concert organized by Take That's Gary Barlow. Performers featured Stevie Wonder (Will.i.am), Grace Jones (Grace Jones), and Kylie Minogue (Minogue).

After the concert, communities and individuals across the United Kingdom, the Channel Islands, the Isle of Man, and other Commonwealth countries lit 2,012 beacons. The Queen lit the National Beacon.

To cap off the weekend's events, Queen Elizabeth II hosted a Diamond Jubilee Day celebration in central London, which included a church service in St Paul's Cathedral, followed by receptions at the Royal Exchange and Westminster Hall, a carriage procession to Buckingham Palace, and a Balcony appearance, flyover, and Feu de Joie.

The Queen's Diamond Jubilee Trust was created to accept donations from anyone who wanted to provide a gift to the monarch during her Diamond Jubilee year. Some of the money that was raised has gone to programs like Queen's Young Leaders, which helps young people all throughout the

Commonwealth who are breaking new ground in their neighborhoods.

The 80th Birthday Celebrations For Her Majesty Queen Elizabeth II

The Queen celebrated her 80th birthday on June 17th, 2006, the day after she turned 80 on April 21st. Several activities were held to commemorate Her Majesty's birthday, which fell on the 21st of April this year, as well as her formal birthday, which fell on the 17th of June.

At Buckingham Palace, a special party for children was held to honor the magic of books. A total of 2,000 youngsters were invited, and the stage performance was carried live on BBC, during which The Queen appeared as a cameo.

A spectacular flypast and a "feu de joie" (fire of joy) were incorporated into the customary celebrations of Trooping the Colour to honor Her Majesty's official birthday.

At St. George's Chapel in Windsor and St. Paul's Cathedral in London, thanksgiving services were held, the latter of which was followed by a lunch at the nearby Mansion House.

At Her Majesty's 'Service over sixty' reception, which honored guests over the age of sixty who have made significant contributions to national life and the Help the Aged Living Legends Awards at Windsor Castle, the Queen joined other members of her generation who had similarly led lives of service and dedication. Those turning 80 on the same day as she was also invited to Buckingham Palace on April 19th.

A special family meal at Kew Palace was followed by a spectacular fireworks display to celebrate the Queen's 88th birthday on her actual birthday. Birthday greetings from the public totaled around 40,000 for Her Majesty's 80th year on Earth.

Her Majesty's 90th birthday celebrations

On the second of three days of national celebrations, the Queen turned 90 years old on April 21, 2016, and on June 11, 2016, she officially celebrated her birthday.

While in Windsor, Her Majesty met well-wishers and others celebrating their 90th birthdays during a town-center walkabout, before dedicating a plaque honoring The Queen's Walkway. To mark the occasion, Her Majesty and HRH The Prince of Wales ignited the country's largest beacon, which was followed by hundreds of smaller ones all over the globe.

Queen Elizabeth II and Prince Philip attended a National Thanksgiving Service at St. Paul's Cathedral on June 10, 2016. Her Majesty's life and function were depicted in prayer at the service. Sir David Attenborough recently finished reading Michael Bond's autobiography, "Growing Up to Be 90," the man who created Paddington Bear.

Her Majesty was joined by members of her family for the Queen's Birthday Parade on Horse

Guards Parade on June 11, 2016, the Queen's formal birthday. Her Majesty then appeared on the balcony of Buckingham Palace for a Flypast.

The Patron's Lunch, a celebration of the Queen's patronage of more than 600 charities and organizations, was held in the Mall on June 12th, 2016.

Her Majesty's good health, unrelenting activity, sharp wit, and leadership of her family, nation, and Commonwealth were all mentioned by the Duke of Cambridge in his homage to his 'Granny.'

Sixty-five years after her coronation, the Queen celebrated her Sapphire Jubilee on February 6, 2017, being the first British monarch to do so.

Buckingham Palace re-released a David Bailey portrait of the monarch taken in 2014 to mark the occasion. The Queen wears a set of sapphire jewelry that King George VI gave her for her wedding in 1947.

Interests

Although she is the Head of State, the Queen manages to fit in time for hobbies and interests outside of her official duties. Her two favorite animals are horses and dogs, which she has adored since she was a child.

As a horse enthusiast, the Queen has a deep understanding of the subject. Epsom's Derby, one of the most prestigious flat races in the United Kingdom, and Ascot's Summer Race Meeting, which has been a Royal event since 1911, are two of her favorite annual outings.

Her Majesty, as a thoroughbred owner and breeder, frequently attends horse races and equestrian events as a spectator.

At Royal Ascot, the Queen's horses have won races on numerous occasions. On the 18th of June 1954, Landau won the Rous Memorial Stakes and a stallion named Aureole won the Hardwicke Stakes, completing a historic double. In 1957, The Queen had four Ascot week winners.

Additionally, the Queen enjoys going on country walks with her pets. The Queen received a Corgi named Susan as a birthday present for her eighteenth birthday, and she has since bred many more of these dogs. Princess Margaret's dog Pipkin was a 'Dorgi,' a cross between a Corgi and a dachshund. Since then, the Queen has kept both Corgis and Dorgis.

Scottish country dance is a lesser-known pastime of mine. When the Queen visits Balmoral Castle, she hosts a series of dances known as "Gillies' Balls" for the benefit of the residents, workers, and visitors of the estate and castle.

Monarchy's Longest Continuity

The Queen became Britain's longest-reigning monarch on September 9th, 2015.

When The Queen and Prince Philip rode a steam train from Edinburgh to Tweedbank to officially open the new Scottish Borders Railway, the occasion was treated as any other. However, in her speech, she did mention the milestone, saying:

"On this occasion, Prince Philip and I would like to express our appreciation for the warm reception you have given us. As First Minister, I'd like to take this opportunity to thank everyone who has pointed out another significance of today. My own life has had many defining moments, and I'm sure yours will as well. Please know that I appreciate all of the good words I've received from friends and family both here in the United States and throughout the world."

Chapter 3

Itinerary For The Platinum Jubilee Festivities

Here we go: the Platinum Jubilation weekend is here. The Queen and other members of the Royal Family were in attendance at today's Trooping the Colour in central London.

Her Majesty The Queen became the first British monarch to celebrate a Platinum Jubilee, celebrating 70 years of service to the people of the United Kingdom, the Realms, and the Commonwealth, on February 6th this year.

A number of magnificent events will take place in central London throughout the four-day UK bank holiday weekend from Thursday 2nd to Sunday 5th June to commemorate this unique occasion. To learn more about what's going on and how you can participate, simply select a day from the calendar.

Additionally, there will be a slew of local events going place across the country.

The 2nd of June

Colorful Trooping

The celebrations for Her Majesty's Diamond Jubilee have begun! A large crowd gathered on London's The Mall and on surrounding huge screens to see Trooping the Colour, while many more watched from their own homes.

Over 1200 officers and troops from the Household Division put on a military spectacle on Horse Guards Parade, together with hundreds of Army musicians and around 240 horses, to parade the 'Colour' or regimental flag. It's been more than 260 years since the British Sovereign's formal birthday was commemorated with this annual celebration. A Royal Gun Salute was fired throughout the procession.

As soon as the parade was over, the Royal Procession returned to Buckingham Palace, where Queen Elizabeth II was joined by The Duke of Kent, Colonel of the Scots Guards, before taking a salute on the balcony of the palace.

Other members of the Royal Family were also on hand to observe the flypast of 70 RAF planes.

Candles With A Platinum Jubilee

What's going on here? The United Kingdom, Channel Islands, Isle of Man, and UK Overseas Territories will light more than 1,500 beacons to commemorate the Queen's Jubilee, Wedding, and Coronation, maintaining the country's ancient tradition of lighting a chain of lights across the country on these occasions.

As a means of communication, a beacon chain has evolved into a sign of solidarity that can be seen at every outdoor gathering or celebration, regardless of the location. The Diamond Jubilee of Queen Victoria was marked in 1897 by the lighting of beacons. Her Majesty's 90th birthday was marked by beacons in 1977, 2002, and 2012 in honor of her Silver and Golden Jubilees, respectively.

A ceremony will be held for the lighting of The Tree of Trees (a 21-meter-tall 'tree' made of 350 smaller trees), which will be lit. Around 9.25 pm, members of the Royal Family will arrive.

Depending on the type of event, there are three options:

1. The UK, Channel Islands, Isle of Man, and UK Overseas Territories will light hundreds of beacons lighted by communities, charities, and other groups. All of the Commonwealth's 54 capital cities will have illuminated beacons.
2. A special ceremony will be held at Buckingham Palace on June 2nd to light the "Principal Beacon."
3. Service of Thanksgiving on Friday, June 3rd.

What's going on here? In honor of Her Majesty's reign, St Paul's Cathedral will host a service of thanksgiving. During the service, the nation's largest church bell, Great Paul, will be rung. It was built in 1882, but a damaged mechanism in the 1970s caused it to go silent. It was restored in 2021 and rang eight times since, but today is the first time it will be rung for a royal occasion.

Members of the Royal Family are expected to begin arriving at around 11 a.m.

June 4th

Epsom Downs Hosts The Derby.

The Derby will be attended by members of the Royal Family at Epsom Downs. English racing's five Classics, the Derby is one of them, with the Oaks, the 2,000 Guineas, St. Leger, and the 1,000 Guineas. Epsom Downs, the venue of the Derby, has a one-mile, four-furlong, and ten-yard race.

A Royal Platinum Ball at Buckingham Palace

What's going on here? Live coverage of the Platinum Party at the Palace will be hosted by Kirsty Young and Roman Kemp and will be broadcast on BBC One, BBC iPlayer, and the BBC network. The Queen's 70-year reign will be celebrated with a night of musical tributes from some of the world's best-known entertainers. A total of 22,000 people are expected to attend, with 10,000 of those tickets distributed through a public ballot and 5,000 reserved for senior staff.

Timings: Around 7.40 pm, members of the Royal Family will arrive. Live coverage of the concert will be available on BBC1 from 8:00 p.m. to 10:30 p.m. on Friday, April 12.

What to look for:

You can watch live on BBC One or catch up on BBC iPlayer from the comfort of your own home.

Watching in public on a large screen: The following sites have large screens where you may see the game:

- The park is located in St. James's, London.
- London's The Mall
- In the city of Cardiff, Bute Park
- Charlotte Square and Royal Botanic
- Garden, Edinburgh

On Sunday, June 5th.

Jubilee Lunch, a Big Deal

The Platinum celebration weekend will see over 60k individuals register to host Big Jubilee Lunches. Activities will range from world record aspirations for the longest street party to backyard BBQs and everything in between.

More than 10 million people are anticipated to participate in Big Jubilee Lunches around the UK as part of a nationwide act of community camaraderie to celebrate the Queen's Diamond Jubilee. Jubilee celebrations are taking place all around the world, from Canada to Brazil, New Zealand to Japan, and

Switzerland to South Africa - with over 600 worldwide Big Jubilant Lunches scheduled.

The Pageant of the Platinum Jubilee

The Pageant will provide a chance for the community to come together and honor Her Majesty. God Save the Queen will be sung, and a gospel choir will sing, to the accompaniment of the Band of Her Majesty's Royal Marine.

The Pageant will bring to life some of the most memorable moments of the Queen's reign, as well as highlight how our society has evolved over the past 70 years.

More than 6,000 volunteers, performers, crucial staff, and 2,500 members of the general public make up the 10,000-strong cast and crew.

These people are coming together from all corners of Britain and the Commonwealth in order to put on a spectacular celebration to commemorate this historic occasion. The 'People's

Pageant' will resonate with people across the United Kingdom.

The Pageant will feature a wide range of national treasures and iconic people from music, movies, sport, and the arts, as well as military troops, essential workers, and volunteers.

At her 70th birthday pageant in 2018, the Gold State Carriage will be led by The Sovereign's Escort as she travels through New York City on her way to being anointed the Queen of England.

Even though Her Majesty will not be riding in the majestic Gold State Carriage, she will be treated to a special treat. The magic of Coronation Day will be re-created utilizing footage taken on that historic day.

Beginning at 2:30 p.m., the Pageant will take place in its entirety.

What to look for:

Watch live on BBC One from 1 pm or catch up on BBC iPlayer from the comfort of your own home.

Watching in public on a large screen: The following sites have large screens where you may see the game:

- London's The Mall.
- The park is located in St. James's, London.
- London's Whitehall
- In the city of Cardiff, Bute Park
- Charlotte Square and Royal Botanic Garden, Edinburgh.

Chapter 4

What Is Trooping The Colors, And Why Does It Matter?

Trooping the Colors has been a tradition for more than 260 years to honor the formal birthday of the British monarch

There are almost 1400 soldiers and 200 horses and 400 musicians who put on a spectacular show every June to celebrate the Queen's formal birthday.

As the procession makes its way from Buckingham Palace along The Mall to Horse Guard's Parade, the streets are crowded with people waving flags.

Members of the Royal Family watch a flyover from Buckingham Palace's balcony at the end of the display.

During Trooping The Colors, What Exactly Happens?

With a Royal salute and an inspection of the troops at Horse Guards Parade in Whitehall, the Queen is received by a group of fully-trained and operational soldiers in ceremonial attire.

The Queen used to ride in a horse-drawn carriage, but she no longer does so.

The Regimental Colour, or banner, is paraded down the ranks of soldiers once the military bands have finished playing. As many as one hundred commanding words are used by the Parade's Officer in Chief to guide the troops in the parade.

At Buckingham Palace, the Queen rides back with the soldiers after the Foot Guards have marched past her, and she then salutes them again.

Members of the Royal Family are then gathered on the balcony of Buckingham Palace for a flyover by the Royal Air Force. The occasion is marked by a 41-gun salute in Green Park.

Chapter 5

The Queen's Six Leadership Lessons

Her Majesty Queen Elizabeth II would be an excellent author for a best-selling self-help book because of her extensive leadership experience spanning over 70 years. Her priorities are clear, and I don't blame her for that.

Since she won't be disclosing any of her insider information, six leadership gurus weigh in on what we may glean from the 96-year-old British monarch:

1. Serving As A Leader

The Queen's leadership approach is best exemplified by Sandhurst's motto: serve to lead. This concept is based on the premise that leadership is an act of service – serving the people you lead and serving the objective that you are collectively working towards". A leadership style that focuses on people and the goal is known as "outward-facing"

During World War II, the Queen apprenticed as a truck mechanic and has dedicated her life to helping others. 30 years after the age of state retirement, he says, "she's still working, meeting people, encouraging their efforts, and promoting the country. I just had the pleasure of meeting her and was amazed by how patient and interested she always is when connecting with individuals."

2. Pursue Your Life's Work.

The Queen, in contrast to most of us, isn't searching for meaning in her life. Since her uncle, Edward VIII, abdicated in 1936, she has been painfully aware of her mission. In addition, her sense of purpose shines through in everything she does, whether it's opening parliament, entertaining presidents, or welcoming community leaders to a garden party.

A clinical psychologist and workplace wellbeing expert, Anna Eliatamby, argue that Queen Elizabeth II has always known and loved her purpose, no matter what the issue, circumstances, or personal cost was, since her coronation in 1947. This has not detracted her from her dedication to her goal - the institution of royalty, family, and obligation towards the people. It's possible that she erred and compromised in some way.

3. Maintain A Positive Outlook In The Face Of Adversity.

Elizabeth II's reign has seen war and peace, economic boom and bust, and even a global pandemic. She has also faced family scandals and personal losses during this time. In total, she has served as prime minister for 14 British governments. A few months shy of his 100th birthday, she lost her husband, Prince Philip, to cancer last year. Despite this, she returned to work just a few days following his death.

A toxic work environment is the No. 1 reason people quit their jobs, In the last 70 years, the Queen has showed how to govern with resilience in the face of severe change and uncertainty, according to her.

When faced with adversity, the Queen has both "pushed through" and "changed course or revised her approach" - all of which are key components of psychological resilience.

4. As The Last Step, Work Together.

Being the Queen may appear to be a one-woman show, but it's actually a team effort that requires a lot of cooperation. When it comes to royal protocol, "the Queen surrounds herself with counsel".

Working with others, she makes decisions together and delegated duty to her family members rather than doing everything herself.

It is said that "a strong leader always has the right mindset and communicates well with others." Teamwork and making the most of others' knowledge and experience are the keys to success."

5. **Authenticity Is The Key To Success.**

The face of Queen Elizabeth II is widely considered to be the most recognizable in the world. She is also well-known for her stylish and individualistic sense of fashion. This includes her demeanor, what she says, and, most importantly, what she wears. She's done an excellent job creating her own brand over her 70-year reign." Self-awareness is a strong attribute of her character.

"If you want to be an authentic leader, you have to look at the internal (how you show up) and the external (whether how you appear to others reflects who you are)," she continues. Your entire potential can be realized when your internal and exterior environments are in harmony.

6. The Importance Of Mental Health And Well-Being Is Not To Be Underestimated

In spite of her famous stoicism, the Queen does not take her mental health for granted. The Queen takes care of her own mental health by balancing work and life (making time for walking her Corgis, visiting her horses, and eating raspberry jam sandwiches).

"The Queen's neurotransmitters remain turning over because she keeps herself active and continues to learn,". This emotion is amplified for her due to the fact that her work is both meaningful and purposeful.

Chapter 6

As the head of state in fifteen countries, Queen Elizabeth II has an international reach. The question is, what does that imply?

In addition to the United Kingdom, Queen Elizabeth II reigns over a total of fourteen other countries. There is renewed discussion about the future of the Crown following Barbados's transition to a republic.

As the longest-serving queen in British history, Queen Elizabeth II took the throne at the age of 25 in 1952. In addition, she reigns over a slew of sovereign states that were British colonies. It was in 2021 that Barbados became the latest country to cut ties with the British Crown. Is this a trend that will spread?

Where Is The Throne Held By Queen Elizabeth II?

There are fourteen additional countries where Queen Elizabeth serves as a queen, including Canada and others in the Caribbean and the Asia-Pacific region. The Commonwealth realms are a group of countries. In contrast to the Commonwealth of Nations, a loose collection of fifty-four countries that were part of the British Empire but are no longer under the queen's authority, these countries are not members of the British Empire.

Moreover, half a billion people live in the Commonwealth countries, the largest of which are the United Kingdom, Canada, Australia, and Papua New Guinea.

What Are The Queen's Broad Powers?

A constitutional monarchy, such as those seen in the Commonwealth, devolves authority away from the king and places it in the hands of elected parliaments and prime ministers. There are no day-to-day responsibilities for the monarchy's head of government, therefore she is only the head of state, not the head of government. There is no head of state or government in Russia, unlike in the United States.

The queen has a few constitutional tasks, the most important of which is the ratification of the new government. For example, she may formally approve laws, nominate officials, or award state accolades depending on the country. The queen selects a royal representative to carry out these responsibilities outside of the United Kingdom. A governor-general has this position.

The Crown also has "reserve powers," or the authority to override the other departments of government unilaterally, in extraordinary circumstances. Australia's 1975 constitutional crisis, in which the governor-general ousted a prime minister, is the most significant incident of this since World War II.

To begin with, the queen serves as a nonpartisan symbol of the nation, continuity of the constitution, and moral authority; official documents are frequently sealed with a royal seal, and local money bears a portrait of the queen as its face.

It is because of her frequent visits to Commonwealth countries like Jamaica, where the republican movement is strong, that people have grown fond of and loyal to the Queen. However, Meghan Markle's claims that the Royal Family is racist have impacted the British government's soft power and diplomatic influence in some areas.

The destiny of the other Commonwealth countries is anyone's guess.

Other Caribbean nations, particularly those in the Caribbean, have recently begun to reexamine their links to the queen in light of Barbados' decision.

Protests in the UK have often focused on the consequences of slavery in British Caribbean colonies and the role it played in the empire's wealth and global power as part of the Black Lives Matter movement that swept the world in 2020. Barbados and other CARICOM members have pressed European governments to make full reparations for their involvement in the slave trade, and some British companies have pledged to do so.

It's no secret that a growing number of people in Jamaica are trying to break away from the monarchy and demand compensation for the Crown's role in the transatlantic slave trade. This decision was made in March 2022, when Jamaican Prime Minister Andrew Holness announced the country's intention to become completely independent of the monarchy.

The chance that other countries will reject the Crown varies widely among analysts. "Barbados could be a turning point," says Kings College historian Richard Drayton. Even yet, according to Professor Aaron Kamugisha of the Barbados' University of the West Indies, the adjustment will have only a limited impact, especially in countries with more stringent criteria.

For example, a constitutional revision in Canada would necessitate the unanimous consent of all 10 provinces and parliament. Since last year, the percentage of Canadians who favor republicanism has risen substantially. The popularity of Queen Elizabeth II is also an influence in Canada and other countries. Observers argue that she commands a level of respect that hasn't yet been achieved by the rest of the royal family, creating a degree of uncertainty for her succession.

Chapter 7

Ancestry of the British Royal Family

The reign of Queen Elizabeth II is the longest in the British monarchy. She has four daughters, eight grandchildren, and a dozen great-grandchildren in her family. The Duke of Edinburgh, her late husband, passed away on April 9th, 2021, at the age of 99. In 1947, five years before she became Queen, the prince married Princess Elizabeth.

You may find out more about the Royal Family and the line of succession below:

The Queen and Prince Philip are two members of the Royal Family. The Queen has been the monarch of the United Kingdom for nearly 70 years.

Princess Elizabeth was born in 1926 and became queen in 1952 when her father, King George VI, died. Since her 1947 union with the Duke of

Edinburgh's son Philip, she has been blessed with a family of four.

He was born in 1921 and served in the British Royal Navy during World War II as a naval aviator. After more than 22,000 solo engagements, he was the longest-serving consort of any British monarch and retired from royal responsibilities in 2017.

On April 9th, 2021, he died.

Conclusion

Succession Path

1. Prince Charles was born in 1948.

The Prince of Wales, Queen Elizabeth II's eldest son and presumed heir, is first in line to the throne.

Diana, Princess of Wales was born Princess of Wales on 29 July 1981 after her marriage to Prince Charles. William and Harry were born to the couple. In 1996, they divorced after being apart for a time. The princess was murdered in a vehicle accident in Paris on August 31st, 1997.

In 2005, on April 9, Prince Charles and Camilla Parker Bowles were married in St. George's Chapel at Windsor Castle. Prince William's primary responsibility is to support the Queen in her duties as heir apparent.

2. Princess Eugenie, Duchess of York, 1982

Second in line to the throne is Prince William, the oldest son of Prince Charles and Princess Diana.

When the duke's mother died, he was just 15 years old. He continued his education at St Andrews University, where he met Kate Middleton, the woman he would eventually marry. It was 2011 when the pair wed.

Counselor of State: He was given this title on his 21st birthday and was expected to act in the Queen's place when she was absent. Among the three of them, George arrived in the summer of 2013, Charlotte followed in 2015, and Louis arrived in the summer of 2018.

The prince served as an RAF search-and-rescue pilot at RAF Valley on Anglesey, north Wales, for three years before becoming a member of the Royal Navy. In addition to his royal duties, he also worked part-time with the East Anglian Air Ambulance for two years. Due to additional royal duties on behalf of the monarchy, he stepped down from the position in July 2017.

3. Prince George, Duke Of Cambridge's Son And Heir Apparent

Born in 2013

At St Mary's Hospital in London, Prince George of Cambridge was born on July 22, 2013. Prince William was on hand to witness the birth of his son, a healthy 8lb 6oz for the princely pair (3.8kg). In the fall of 2017, he began kindergarten.

After his father and grandfather, Prince George is third in line to the throne.

4. The Duchess of Cambridge, Charlotte

In 2015, he was born.

Her second child, a girl, was born on May 2, 2015, at St Mary's Hospital in London. The 8lb 3oz (3.7kg) baby was delivered in front of the Duke of Cambridge. Charlotte Elizabeth Diana was the royal baby's given name by her parents, the Duke and Duchess of Cambridge.

Her Royal Highness Princess Charlotte of Cambridge is the fourth in line to the throne of the United Kingdom.

5. The Prince of Cambridge's son, Prince Louis

Date of Birth: 2018

At St Mary's Hospital in London, the Duchess of Cambridge gave birth to her third child, a boy weighing 8lbs 7oz, on April 23, 2018.

Louis Arthur Charles was born in front of the Duke and Duchess of Cambridge.

6. The Duke of Sussex, Prince Harry

Born in 1984

Prince Harry completed his military training at the Royal Military Academy Sandhurst and was commissioned as a lieutenant in the Army.

As a co-pilot and gunner of an Apache chopper, Capt Wales served in Afghanistan twice during his ten years in the military. He retired from the military in 2015 and now devotes his time to charity causes, including conservation in Africa and coordinating the Invictus Games for injured members of the military.

Since the age of 21, he has served as a Counsellor of State, acting as the Queen's representative in official capacities.

On the 19th of May, 2018, he married actress Meghan Markle at Windsor Castle. Toward the end of 2019, the Duke and Duchess of Cambridge announced that they would step back from their roles as "Senior Royals" in order to spend more time in the United Kingdom and North America. These people claimed to be working toward financial independence as one of their stated goals.

Soon after, Buckingham Palace announced that the Duke and Duchess of Cambridge would not be returning to their royal duties and would relinquish their honorary military postings and royal patronages.

7. Archie Harrison Mountbatten-Winsor

Date of Birth: 2019

Archie Harrison Mountbatten-Windsor, the couple's first child, was born on May 6th, weighing in at 7 pounds, 3 ounces, with the duke in attendance. The couple decided not to give their first child a title by naming him as they did.

Jonny Dymond, a BBC royal journalist, said the choice was a strong signal that the couple did not wish to raise him as an official royal.

8. Diana Mountbatten-daughter Windsor's Lilibet

In 2021, he was born.

Her second child was born on June 4th, 2021, in Santa Barbara, California to the Duchess of Sussex and Prince Harry. As the 11th great-grandchild of the Queen, Lilibet Diana Mountbatten-Windsor is named after the Royal Family's nickname for her.

Because of Prince Harry's mother, who died tragically in a car accident in 1997 when the prince was 12, was given the middle name Diana.

9. **The Duke Of York**

Born in 1960

The Duke Of York Is the son of Queen Elizabeth II and Prince Philip. For the first time in 103 years, the Queen and Duke of Edinburgh gave birth to an heir to the throne, Prince Andrew.

When he married Sarah Ferguson, the future Duchess of York, in 1986, he became the Duke of York. Eugenie was born in 1990, while Beatrice was born in 1988. Announcing the duke and duchess' separation was made in March 1992. In 1996, they called it quits.

The duke served in the Royal Navy for 22 years and participated in the 1982 Falklands War. Until 2011, he also served as the government's special trade representative, in addition to his royal duties.

Prince Andrew stepped away from royal duties in 2019 after an interview with the BBC regarding his involvement with US businessman Jeffrey Epstein, who murdered himself while awaiting prosecution on sex trafficking and conspiracy charges.

The duke was strongly condemned for his association with Epstein, but he stated he did not notice any suspicious behavior during trips to the US financier's residence.

In a statement, saying he was stepping back from public obligations for the foreseeable future, the duke said he strongly regretted his "ill-judged association with Jeffrey Epstein".

10.   Princess Beatrice

Born: 1988

Princess Beatrice is the oldest daughter of Prince Andrew and Sarah, Duchess of York. Her full name is Princess Beatrice of York, and she is the Royal

Highness of the United Kingdom. She has no official surname but uses the name York.

She married property tycoon Edoardo Mapelli Mozzi at The Royal Chapel of All Saints at Royal Lodge, Windsor, in July 2020. The pair had been supposed to marry in May, but coronavirus postponed the preparations.

In September 2021, Princess Beatrice gave birth to a daughter, Sienna Elizabeth, who will be the 11th in line to the throne and the 12th great-grandchild of Queen Elizabeth II. Christopher Woolf, also known as Wolfie, is the son of Mr. Mapelli Mozzi and Dara Huang's previous relationship, and he has Princess Beatrice as a stepmother.

11.   Princess Eugenie

Born: 1990

Princess Eugenie is Prince Andrew and Sarah, Duchess of York's youngest daughter. Elizabeth II's

12th in line to the throne has given her the title "Her Royal Highness Princess Eugenie of York."

The name "York" is her surname, like that of her sister, Princess Beatrice. On October 12, 2018, she married her longtime boyfriend, Jack Brooksbank, at Windsor Castle.

12.   Philip Brooksbank Hawkesworth

He was born in the year 2021.

The ninth great-grandchild of Queen Elizabeth II will be born on February 9, 2021, to Princess Eugenie and Jack Brooksbank.

13.   Earl Of Wessex

When Prince Edward married his longtime girlfriend, Sophie, he was crowned Earl of Wessex and Viscount Severn. James, Viscount Severn was born in 2007 and Lady Louise (their first child) was born in 1964.

After serving in the Royal Marines for a short time, the prince decided to start his own production firm for television shows. As part of his new role, he helps the Queen with her formal responsibilities and makes public appearances on behalf of charities. As a result of the birth of Princess Beatrice's daughter in September, he is now 14th in line to the throne.

14.   Countess of Severn, Viscount James

Born in the year of 2007

The Earl and Countess of Wessex have a younger son, Viscount Severn, who is the Viscount of Severn. As a courtesy, boys and daughters of aristocratic lords were not granted the more official titles of prince or princess. Because of the constraints of royal titles, it is believed that this decision was made.

15.   Lady Louise

Was born in 2003.

She was born in 2003 to the Earl and Countess of Weymouth, Lady Louise Windsor.

16.   The Princess Royal

Born in the year 1950

Anne Princess Royal is the Queen's only daughter and her second child. When she was born, she was ranked third in line to the throne, but currently, she is ranked 17th in line. In June of that year, she was given the title "Princess Royal."

Her two children, Peter and Zara, were born to her first husband, Captain Mark Phillips, and their second spouse, Vice-Admiral Timothy Laurence.

During her marriage to Captain Phillips, the princess became the first royal to use the surname Mountbatten-Windsor in a legal document such as a marriage certificate. Since 1970, she has served as president of Save the Children, an organization she has been a part of since its inception. She represented the United Kingdom in equestrian competitions at the 1976 Montreal Olympics.

17. Peter Phillips

Born in 1977

Peter Phillips is the Queen's oldest grandson. When he and Canadian Autumn Kelly got married two years later in 2008, they had a daughter named Savannah and a daughter named Isla two years later in 2012.

Because they are descended from a female line, Princess Royal's offspring do not hold royal titles. For the sake of their children, Mark Phillips rejected the offer of an earldom when he wed.

In February 2020, Peter Phillips and his wife announced their separation.

18. Savannah Phillips

Date of Birth: 2010

Peter and Autumn Phillips had their first child, a great-granddaughter named Savannah, in 2010.

19.   Isla Phillips

2012 was the year of birth .

Isla Phillips was born to Peter and Autumn Phillips in 2012.

20.   Zara Tindall

Born in 1981

Ms. Phillips

Following in the footsteps of her famously successful parents, Zara Tindall rode to a silver medal at the Olympics in London in 2012. In 2014, she and Mike Tindall welcomed their first child, Mia Grace. A year later, she married the ex-England rugby player.

Princess Royal's children do not hold a royal title because they are descended from the female line, but she remains 21st in line to the throne. There are no courtesy titles for the Phillips children because their father, Mark Phillips, rejected an earldom when he wed Princess Anne.

21.   Mia Grace Tindall.

Born in 2014

Tindall's daughter

Zara Tindall, the granddaughter of Queen Elizabeth II, gave birth to her first child in January.

22.   Lena Elizabeth Tindall

As of 2018, Lena Elizabeth was born.

On June 18, 2018, at Stroud Maternity Unit, Gloucestershire, the Queen's seventh great-grandchild was born. Named after her great-grandmother, Lena Elizabeth.

Lena Elizabeth, like her sister, does not hold a royal title and will therefore be referred to as Miss Tindall, like her sister.

Made in the USA
Monee, IL
13 September 2022

13895701R00046